COUNTING HEADS, AND MORE

COUNTING HEADS, AND MORE

The Work of the U.S. Census Bureau

By Marta E. McCave

FOR MY PARENTS, WHO HAVE SPENT COUNTLESS HOURS STUDYING
CENSUS ARCHIVES IN THEIR SEARCH FOR FAMILY ANCESTORS.

Many thanks to former Commerce Department Under Secretary Everett M. Ehrlich, Debbi Barrett of
the Census Bureau's Public Information Office; David M. Pemberton, Decennial Census Historian;
and Ann Domski, senior field representative for the U.S. Census Bureau in the Philadelphia region.

Library of Congress Cataloging-in-Publication Data

McCave, Marta E.
Counting heads, and more: the work of the U.S. Census Bureau / Marta E. McCave.
p. cm.
Includes bibliographical references and index.
Summary: Describes how the census is accomplished, examines its history, and discusses its far-
reaching impact on every facet of government and business.
ISBN 0-7613-3017-8 (lib. bdg.)
1. United States. Bureau of the Census—History—Juvenile literature. 2. United States—Statistical
services—History—Juvenile literature. 3. United States—Census—History—Juvenile Literature.
[1.United States. Bureau of the Census. 2. United States—Census.] I.Title.
HA37.U55M313 1998
352.7'5'0973—DC21
97-51643   CIP   AC

Cover design by Linda Kosarin
Interior design by Claire Fontaine

Photographs courtesy of Photo Researchers: pp. 8 (© 1997 Ken Cavanagh); Library of Congress: p.
21; Corbis-Bettmann: p. 23, United States Department of Commerce, Bureau of the Census: pp. 24,
26, 31; The Stock Market: pp. 45 (top left, © 1993 Jose Fuste Raga; top right, © 1995 Richard Beren-
holtz; center © 1989 Donald C. Johnson; bottom left © 1995 Joe Sohm), 59 (© 1994 John Henley);
Gamma Liaison: pp. 47 (© 1997 Steven Burr Williams), 52 (© Diana Walker); Stock, Boston (© Mark
Burnett)

Published by Twenty-First Century Books
A Division of The Millbrook Press
2 Old New Milford Road
Brookfield, Connecticut 06804

CONTENTS

1

A VISIT FROM
THE CENSUS
BUREAU

"Official business," said the letter your family received from the U.S. Census Bureau one day. It notified you that your household had been selected to participate in something called the Current Population Survey. The letter said you would be participating in a very important process, and your answers would be kept in strictest confidence.

So you are not too surprised when a stranger with a Census Bureau identification badge and a laptop computer knocks on the door one evening. As she is invited in, you wonder what it will be like to play a role in an important government survey.

The Census Bureau field representative sits at your kitchen table, asking the adults (that is, anyone 15 or older) a series of questions that she reads from a computer screen. She clicks away on her computer keyboard as she inputs their answers.

"Last week did you do any work for pay?" she asks. "How many hours did you work last week?"

The Census Bureau conducts more than 100 surveys a year. The gentleman at left is being asked a few questions by a Census Bureau field representative.

She asks whether the worker is employed by the government, a private company, a nonprofit organization, or is self-employed. She carefully types in the name of the employer, the type of industry, and the type of work the person does. And she asks how much money the worker earned in the last 12 months. Those are just some of the questions that are asked.

You wonder why the government needs to know some things. "Last week did you lose or take off any hours from work for any reason, such as illness, slack work, vacation, or holiday?" the representative wants to know.

If the workers are not currently employed, the Census Bureau representative asks a different set of questions. Suppose a member of the household has been laid off. "Has your employer given you a date to return to work?" the Census Bureau representative asks. "Have you been given any indication that you will be called to work within the next six months?"

Perhaps someone in the household is looking for work. "What are all of the things that you have done to find work during the last four weeks?" the field representative asks. Someone who did nothing to seek work is asked, "What are the main reasons that you were not looking for work during the last four weeks?"

Interviews like this are going on in more than 50,000 households throughout the nation during the third week of every month, year in and year out. The Census Bureau selects households randomly according to their addresses.

The Census Bureau will use the information to paint a statistical portrait of the nation's job market—a key indicator of our country's overall economic health. Every question in the survey yields a useful piece of information—even the question about how many hours of work were missed due to illness. Statisticians will use the data to estimate how many Americans do not have jobs, which sectors of the economy are weakest, and other trends that are part of the national employment picture.

The findings will be announced on the first Friday of the following month by the U.S. Labor Department. They will be reported on radio and television and in newspapers and electronic media. Economists will scrutinize the statistics to determine how the employment picture varies from one part of the coun-

FUN FACTS

HOW DOES RACE AFFECT YOUR CHANCES OF FINISHING HIGH SCHOOL?

The proportion of African Americans aged 25 to 29 who had completed high school improved significantly from 1985 to 1995—from 81 percent to 87 percent. The share of young adult whites in the same age group remained unchanged at about 87 percent.

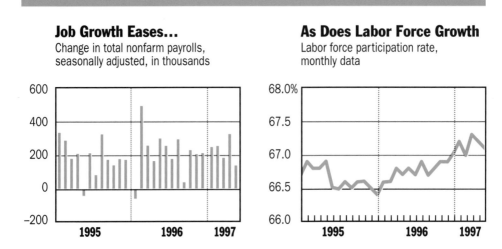

Job Growth Eases...
Change in total nonfarm payrolls, seasonally adjusted, in thousands

As Does Labor Force Growth
Labor force participation rate, monthly data

Newspapers and other media use government statistics, such as these employment figures, to inform the public about changes in economic and social conditions.

try to another or from one category of workers to another. If unemployment is high, it could create pressure on Congress and the president to propose new job programs. If unemployment is low, businesses might start worrying that they will have to pay higher salaries to attract the workers they need.

Just think: All of those important consequences for national growth and prosperity are occurring because of the information the Census Bureau collected from ordinary Americans like your family. Of course, it is the numbers that are in the spotlight. The names of the people who participated in the survey are never mentioned. The news media, the economists, and the government leaders do not even know who the individuals are behind the statistics.

By law, Census Bureau employees must hold all answers in strict confidence. A special computer software program encoded the data so that the personal details that could reveal your family's identity were protected. Shortly after your family was interviewed, the field representative used a modem to transmit the data electronically to the huge mainframe computers at Census Bureau headquarters in Suitland, Maryland. And as soon as the data was sent to headquarters, it was automatically deleted from the laptop computer where it was first recorded—another measure aimed at protecting your privacy.

It may seem like an awful lot of effort for one report. But the work begins all over again the next month. The Census Bureau conducts the employment survey for the Labor Department every month, year in and year out. After your first participation in the survey, you can expect to be contacted every month for the next three months and asked the same sets of questions. Eight months later, you will be interviewed for another four-month period. That provides a longer-term picture of what is happening to workers in the job market.

The Current Population Survey is just one of more than 100 surveys the U.S. Census Bureau conducts every year. Read on to learn about all of the information gathering the Bureau does and how it has earned the nickname, the Nation's Fact-Finder.

2

FACT-FINDER FOR THE NATION

We live in the "information age." We have information at our fingertips in ways the world never knew could be possible. Much of that information is in statistics, or numerical data. The availability of statistics has revolutionized the way governments govern and businesses go about buying and selling. It even shapes the way people make decisions about their lives. From the day you were born, statistics have been gathered about you. If you caught the flu last winter, visited Disney World, or enjoy watching a favorite TV program on Tuesday nights at 8:30 P.M., you can bet there are statistics somewhere that reveal how many other people share the same experience.

When you decide upon a career, you may use statistical information yourself. Although you may have strong feelings about the kind of work you want to do, you still may want to do some research to unearth statistics such as how plentiful jobs are in that field and what the average salaries are.

The U.S. government has been conducting censuses since 1790. In fact, the U.S. Census is the oldest continuously operated census system in the entire world. The Census Bureau calls itself the Nation's Fact-Finder. It collects information by asking questions of households, businesses, and governments. It asks its questions by mail, telephone, or personal visits. The Census Bureau publishes about 2,000 reports a year on a wealth of topics. It also conducts surveys, such as the Current Population Survey described in the first chapter of this book, for other agencies in the federal government. But the Census Bureau is best known for the nationwide head count that it conducts every ten years.

FUN FACTS

HOW MANY PEOPLE WILL GET MARRIED TODAY, AND HOW MANY WILL SPLIT?

In 1994, 2.4 million marriages and 1.2 million divorces took place in the United States. That means 6,500 marriages and 3,300 divorces on a typical day.

THE DECENNIAL

On April 1 of every year ending in zero (such as 1990 or 2000), the Census Bureau asks each household in America to fill out a questionnaire that asks how many people live at that address, how old they are, and other questions about population and housing. The official name of this massive undertaking is the Census of Population and Housing. It is often referred to as the Decennial Census, or simply the Census. Most people receive their questionnaires by mail and return them by mail. But to make sure that the response rate is as complete as possible, Census workers, called enumerators, fan out across the country to personally interview those who did not receive the mailed questionnaire, or who did not return it.

If you think of the Census Bureau as a photographer and the Decennial Census as a snapshot of America at one given moment, here are some of the glimpses the camera gave us in 1990:

✎ The resident population of the United States on April 1, 1990, was 248.7 million, 9.8 percent above the 1980 census count of 226.5 million.

✍ Twenty-four percent of American families with children were one-parent households.

✍ The nation's growth rate had dropped since 1980, partly because of an increasing number of deaths as the population aged.

✍ People 65 years old and over accounted for 12.5 percent of the population, up from 11.3 percent ten years earlier. People under 18 were 25.7 percent of the population, down from 28.1 percent in 1980.

✍ The West had the highest growth rate (22.3 percent) among the four regions of the United States.

✍ The five states with the highest increases in population from 1980 to 1990 were Nevada (50.1 percent), Alaska (36.9 percent), Arizona, (34.9 percent), Florida (32.7 percent), and California (25.7 percent).

WHY A CENSUS?

Today, we think of a census as any official *enumeration*, or counting, of the population that occurs at set intervals. History's earliest censuses were conducted so that taxes could be levied or armies raised. The word "census" comes from the Latin "censere," which means "to tax" or "assess." Ancient census takers counted males of military age, heads of households, and landowners. Women and children were rarely included. The most famous census in history is the one ordered by Caesar Augustus. In the New Testament of the Bible, the Gospel of Luke tells the story of how Joseph and Mary traveled to Bethlehem at the time of Jesus' birth to participate in that census.

Our Constitution calls for a census every ten years so that seats in the House of Representatives can be fairly divided, or *apportioned*, based on the population of the states. However, since the first census was conducted in 1790, uses for the data have broadened. Today, census statistics are used to draw election district lines. Census statistics are also used to distribute billions of dollars a year in government funds for local programs in education, health services, nutrition, day care, crime prevention, and more. And the valuable data are used in many ways by state and local

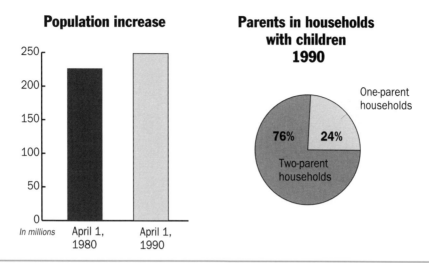

Population increase

250
200
150
100
50
0

In millions   April 1, 1980   April 1, 1990

Parents in households with children 1990

One-parent households

76%   24%

Two-parent households

Population density

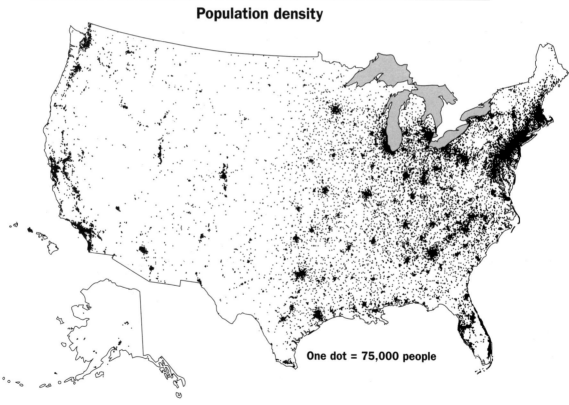

One dot = 75,000 people

Many different types of information about U.S residents can be found by examining census figures.

governments, businesses, academic researchers, nonprofit organizations, the media, and individuals.

No other country in the world collects and publishes as much statistical information as the United States. Some critics say the United States should find a cheaper, simpler way to gather the information it needs about the population. One alternative could be a national population register. Some countries require their people to register with the central government, providing information about their households and events such as births, marriages, and deaths. Belgium, the Netherlands, Switzerland, and the Scandinavian countries are some of the nations that have used population registers to count heads.

Think of a central registry as a sort of national address list. We don't have such a central registry in the United States, and having one could create many problems. Americans are a mobile population; we move around often. It is unlikely that Americans would accept the idea of having to register with the government every time they moved across town or across the country. In addition, we are a nation with a large illegal immigrant population. It would be impossible to get an accurate count of illegal aliens in the United States with a mandatory registration system.

THE BUREAU'S MANY RESPONSIBILITIES

Many Americans think the Census Bureau works only every ten years, when it is time for the Decennial Census. In fact, the Census Bureau is constantly gathering information on birth and death, crime and unemployment, consumer spending and health, and many more facets of life in the United States.

For every year ending in "2" or "7," the Census Bureau conducts specialized censuses that focus on individual economic sectors, including communications, construction, finance, insurance, governments, manufacturing, mining, real estate, retail trade, services, transportation, utilities, and wholesale trade.

One of the most important is the economic census. This census provides a detailed portrait of the nation's economy from the national to the local level. The census has eight major components. For the latest economic census, forms were mailed to more than 3.5 million firms. There were over 500 versions of the form, each customized to various industries. Very small firms were not included.

The Census Bureau also conducts more than 100 surveys a year, such as the Current Population Survey on employment, which was discussed in this book's first chapter. Unlike a census, which aims to count every member of a group or population, a survey examines only a sample of an entire population. Sampling provides a cross section of households, individuals, or special groups. Each sample is scientifically selected so that the results are representative of the whole.

Surveys are conducted monthly, quarterly, and yearly. Here are some of the surveys:

✍ The Consumer Expenditure Survey measures household spending on consumer goods. The survey is done for the Department of Labor's Bureau of Labor Statistics. This is the survey that produces the cost-of-living statistics, another key economic indicator.

✍ The National Crime Victimization Survey measures the effects of crimes on their victims. The survey is done for the Department of Justice and is conducted every six months. This is the survey that produces the crime rate statistics.

✍ The National Health Interview Study gathers information from a sample of the population about illness and disability. The weekly survey is conducted for the Center for Disease Control and the National Center for Health Statistics.

✍ The Survey of the Income and Program Participation measures eligibility and participation in federal assistance programs.

3

THE EARLY
DAYS

The War for Independence was over. The 13 American colonies were now the United States, and the new nation owed huge debts. To figure out how to divide the debt among its people, the government needed to find out how many people it had. The government also needed to count heads to establish a new government as set forth in its Constitution.

Under the Constitution, the U.S. Senate would have two senators for each state. But the House of Representatives would be apportioned, or divided, according to population. Heavily populated states would be entitled to more members in the House of Representatives than smaller states. Here is how the framers of the U.S. Constitution, adopted in 1787, dealt with the problem of apportioning representatives and assessing taxes:

Representatives and direct Taxes shall be apportioned among the several States which may be included within this Union, according to their respec-

tive Numbers. . . . The actual Enumeration shall be made within three Years after the first Meeting of the Congress of the United States, and within every subsequent Term of ten Years, in such Manner as they shall by Law direct. (Article I, Section 2)

The framers of the Constitution had a sound reason for using the census for taxation and apportionment. They believed that it would lead to a more accurate count. If people thought they were being counted only for tax purposes, they wouldn't be as likely to cooperate and the count would be too low. After all, who likes paying taxes? If people were being counted only for purposes of finding out how many members of the House they were entitled to, the states might inflate the numbers so they would have more votes on legislation.

Although constitutionally planned, taxation based on the census count never did occur. But, as history would show, it was fortunate that the census was not limited in the kinds of information it could gather.

THE FIRST U.S. CENSUS

As secretary of state, Thomas Jefferson oversaw the first U.S. Census in 1790. It was not an easy undertaking because the people of the new nation were scattered from Maine to Georgia and westward toward the Mississippi River. In some wilderness areas, there were few roads or bridges.

Each of the 17 U.S. marshals was asked to appoint as many assistants as he needed to take the census. At that time, the Marshals Service was one of the few federal civilian agencies with an organizational network throughout the land. And because it had law-enforcement duties, its marshals would know where people lived.

The census takers were instructed to count white males, free white females, all other free persons, and slaves, all of whom were presumed to be black. They were also to distinguish between free white males 16 or older and those under 16—useful information for the government to have in the event of a war or uprising.

The first census asked only six questions:

✍ name of the head of the family

✍ number of free white males 16 and up

✍ number of free white males under 16

✍ number of free white females

✍ number of slaves

✍ number of all other free persons regardless of gender or race

Because marshals had to furnish their own paper, the information was recorded on all sorts of books and sheets. After covering his assigned area on horseback or on foot, each assistant was required to post a copy of his census "return" in two public places. In that way, everyone could see it and bring errors or omissions to the attention of the authorities.

Most Americans cooperated. But some saw the census as an invasion of their privacy. Having just fought a war over taxation without representation, there were those who suspected any government undertaking that might lead to higher taxes. By law, however, anyone who refused to be counted could be fined $20. Some people were indeed prosecuted for resisting; however, no records that survive reveal whether they actually paid fines.

When the final count was completed after 18 months, the new nation's population stood at 3,893,637. Officials were disappointed by the results. They thought some people had been overlooked. Both

FUN FACTS

WHICH STATE HAS THE MOST PEOPLE?

According to 1996 figures, California is the most populous state with a population of about 31.9 million, followed by Texas, with 19.1 million people; New York, with 18.1 million; and Florida, with 14.4 million.

Thomas Jefferson was in charge of the first U.S. Census in 1790. He later became the third president of the United States.

George Washington and Thomas Jefferson thought that the population should have been more than four million. Washington blamed the "indolence of the people."

Here is what Jefferson said in a letter written on August 29, 1791, to diplomat William Carmichael:

I enclose you also a copy of our census, which, so far as it is written in black ink, is founded upon actual returns, what is in red ink being conjectured, but very near the truth. Making very small allowances for omissions, which we know to have been very great, we may safely say we are above four millions.

MORE PEOPLE, MORE QUESTIONS

As the decades went by, the census added more questions. Social scientists and others realized the census was a valuable opportunity for gathering information on a variety of topics. Census-takers asked people about their jobs, their debts, their military service, their education, their churches, and crime. Clerks tabulated the results using tally marks, or they added up the columns of figures with pen or pencil.

The nation's population was growing by leaps and bounds, increasing the difficulty of the census-taking task. By 1840, the population had grown from 3.9 million to 17 million. The census was becoming too complicated to be carried out by the U.S. Marshals Service. By 1880, there were 233 separate question forms collecting more than 13,000 pieces of information. With workers tallying that data by hand, it took over seven years to publish the results!

An important piece of legislation called the Census Act for 1880 resulted in some improvements. Congress removed census responsibilities from the U.S. Marshals Service and established a temporary census office within the government's Department of Interior. It also created a

FUN FACTS

WHICH STATES ARE THE FASTEST GROWING?

The U.S. population will rise by 72 million people over the next 30 years, to 335 million in 2025. More than 30 million of that increase is expected to occur in just three states: California, Texas, and Florida.

This 1890 magazine illustration shows a man punching cards with an attachment operated by storage batteries. Tabulation machines such as this one helped speed up the processing of census data and were an important forerunner of the computer.

Herman Hollerith invented a tabulating system that used punch cards to record data. Hollerith's invention revolutionized information processing.

system for hiring temporary clerical workers and field-workers to gather the data. Historians say the change improved the accuracy of the 1880 census.

TECHNOLOGY ARRIVES

Thanks to a man named Herman Hollerith, punch cards and electric tabulating equipment came along in time for the 1890 census. Hollerith had worked in the census office. He developed and patented a tabulating system that could count 250 items a minute using cards with holes punched in them at designated places. Each hole in a card recorded a particular bit of information, and as the cards were mechanically fed through the machine, the machine "read" the holes. (Actually, electric current passed through each hole and tripped a counter in the machine.) For example, to indicate a citizen who could read, a card would have a hole punched in column seven, ninth row from the top.

Hollerith built his own tabulating machines and leased them with card-punching and sorting machines to the census. With Hollerith's invention, the 1890 census was able to process census data four times faster than it had in 1880. The invention marked the beginning of a new era in census history. It has also been called the birth of the information processing industry.

Hollerith is in the Inventor's Hall of Fame, but his name is not as widely known as the company he established. In 1896 he founded the Tabulating Machine Company, Inc., which, through later mergers, grew into the International Business Machines Corporation. Most people know it today as IBM.

THE 20TH CENTURY

In the 20th century, the pace of change accelerated and the Bureau of the Census came to resemble the agency it is today. The Bureau of the Census became a permanent government agency in 1902. That meant there would now be a permanent professional census organization instead of one that was assembled anew every ten years. Initially part of the Department of Interior, the Bureau was moved to the

UNIVAC was the first large-scale electronic computer. Used during the 1940s and 1950s, it was so big that it had to be housed in a separate room.

Department of Commerce and Labor in 1905. When Labor was split off from the department in 1913, the Bureau remained with Commerce.

Meanwhile, the Bureau also became much more sophisticated about the way it gathered and processed information. Mechanized punches replaced the hand-operated devices. By the 1920 census, the Bureau was using tabulating machines that could handle five times as many cards as those of 1900. By the 1940 census, the Bureau's tabulating machines could handle 2,000 items a minute, compared to 1890's 250 items a minute.

The greatest technological leap forward came in the 1940s with the development of the first large-scale electronic computer. UNIVAC I (UNIVAC stood for Universal Automatic Computer) was designed and built specifically for the Census Bureau. It could tabulate 4,000 items a minute. Although it was used in census processing in the early 1950s, its usefulness was limited because the process still required labor-intensive coding and card punching, plus transferring the data from cards to computer tape.

Then came FOSDIC (Film Optical Sensing Device for Input to Computers), an electronic device for reading census questionnaires. FOSDIC was designed to read special questionnaires on which the answers were indicated by blackening small circles. In practice, it was used to "read" microfilmed copies of the coded schedules and transfer the data to magnetic tape at speeds up to 70,000 items a minute. Jointly developed by the Census Bureau and the National Bureau of Standards, it eliminated the need for an army of clerks preparing punch cards.

A different kind of milestone came in 1960, when the Census Bureau began to use the mail system for the first time. Mail carriers delivered census questionnaires to housing units across the country. Householders were asked to complete the questionnaire and hold onto it until an enumerator called on them to retrieve it. In the 1970 census, residents were asked to return their questionnaires by mail. Using the mail saved the Bureau a lot of legwork, but thousands of field-workers were still needed to follow up on nonrespondents. And thousands of clerical workers had to process the monumental load of paper census questionnaires.

Someday the census may reach another milestone—an electronic, paperless census. What a long way the census will have come from 1790!

4

THE
CENSUS BUREAU
TODAY

If number crunching gave off smoke like old-time factories did, a huge cloud would be hanging in the air over Suitland, Maryland. That's where the headquarters for the U.S. Census Bureau is located, about four miles (6 kilometers) outside Washington, D.C.

Many of the men and women who are employed by the U.S. Census Bureau work at the Suitland Federal Center, a cluster of government buildings on a sprawling campus. Together with overflow office space nearby, the buildings known as FB3 and FB4 (Federal Buildings #3 and #4) house more than 3,600 workers.

Behind the security gates that surround the Suitland compound, the Census Bureau boasts a worker population that is a village in itself. Broad corridors stretch in many directions, lined with clusters of offices and cubicles tucked away behind closed doors. An underground tunnel links FB3 and FB4. Down the road, a child-care center called Bureautots serves the day-care needs of employees. Shuttles ferry employees and other visitors between Suitland and other government buildings in the District of Columbia.

Thousands of visitors pass through the Suitland Federal Center's security gates every year. Often those visitors are representatives from other nations who want to study some aspect of the United States' census system. China, the world's most populous nation, has consulted with the U.S. Census Bureau on its nationwide decennial census. Since 1946, the Bureau has trained more than 5,600

people from statistical organizations in other parts of the world. In addition, statistical software developed at the Census Bureau is used in some 200 computer centers around the world.

BEYOND HEADQUARTERS

The Census Bureau also maintains 12 regional offices—Atlanta, Georgia; Boston, Massachusetts; Charlotte, North Carolina; Chicago, Illinois; Dallas, Texas; Denver, Colorado; Detroit, Michigan; Kansas City, Kansas; Los Angeles, California; New York, New York; Philadelphia, Pennsylvania; and Seattle, Washington. Those regional offices deal with data collection and offer assistance to data users. There are about 5,700 employees, including more than 3,000 field representatives who do the legwork for surveys and censuses.

In addition, the Bureau operates processing and support facilities in Jeffersonville, Indiana, and Pittsburg, Kansas. At Jeffersonville, the Bureau conducts its clerical, microfilming, and mapmaking operations. It processes incoming data there so it can be analyzed and computer-processed at Suitland.

In Pittsburg, the Bureau houses confidential records such as the microfilm copies of individual population census records. Sometimes people who need official proof of their age and place of birth—to apply for Social Security or to get a passport, for example—ask the Census Bureau for an official transcript of the past census records that contain their vital statistics. The Pittsburg staff issues almost 40,000 official transcripts a year.

WHO WORKS FOR THE BUREAU?

The head of the Bureau is called the director. Appointed by the president and confirmed by the U.S. Senate, the director oversees 35 divisions with the assistance of a deputy director. The director reports to the chief economist of the Department of Commerce.

It takes many people with a wide range of talents to do the work of the Bureau. The Bureau's permanent staff includes statisticians, economists, demographers, and sociologists, plus specialists in information technology, computer programmers, and engineers. People with backgrounds in business administration, finance, personnel, publications, management analysis, and administrative services also play a vital role in the Bureau's operations.

What do all those people do? Demographers, statisticians, and other experts in specific fields determine what information is needed by users and how it can be best presented. They plan the censuses and surveys, develop questionnaires, and analyze the data that results. Geographers help define the geographic statistical areas that will be used in data collection. That includes mapmaking as well as defining statistical areas for the gathering of data. Computer programmers, engineers, and experts in information technology manage the flow of data.

The field representatives employed around the country to collect data for ongoing periodic censuses and surveys are a much more diverse group. Many of them are part-time workers. They come from all walks of life, and some are people who have retired from other careers.

F U N   F A C T S

ARE THERE MORE SINGLE GUYS OR SINGLE GIRLS?

In 1995, there were 118 unmarried men aged 18 to 34 for every 100 unmarried women that age.

More than 3,600 people work in the U.S. Census Bureau's headquarters in Suitland, Maryland. Thousands more work in regional centers around the nation.

The Bureau's workforce balloons every ten years when it is time for the Decennial Census of Population and Housing. Thousands of temporary workers are hired and trained. Most of them are employed for just a few weeks as enumerators or clerical workers. The decennial hiring boom makes the Bureau of the Census unique. No other federal agency has a workforce that fluctuates so widely.

5

DECENNIAL

Every ten years, the U.S. Census Bureau attempts to gather information from every household in the country. The formal name of this undertaking is the Census of Population and Housing, but it could also be called Mission Impossible. The objective is to locate every person and every living quarters in the United States, deliver a questionnaire, and receive a completed one in return.

In 1990, the Census Bureau counted approximately 106 million housing units in the United States, plus people and housing units in Puerto Rico, the U.S. Virgin Islands, Guam, the Commonwealth of the Northern Mariana Islands, American Samoa, and Palau.

Every household in the United States—or individuals in the case of group housing situations like dorms and prisons—is expected to fill out what's known as the "short form" of the census questionnaire. In addition, a smaller number of households are asked to complete a much longer questionnaire known as the "long

"It's OK Boys. You can tell him everything...
He's the Census Man!"

This cartoon was part of the Census Bureau's 1950 publicity campaign.
By emphasizing that residents had nothing to fear by talking to enumerators,
the Bureau hoped to increase participation in the census.

form." In the 1990 Census, about one out of every six households was asked to complete the long form.

THE FOOT SOLDIERS OF THE CENSUS

Census archives are full of wonderful stories from census takers. Until recent decades, when the Bureau began using the mail to send and receive questionnaires, field representatives personally contacted each household. Enumerators have made their rounds on foot, on horseback, by car, outrigger canoe, airplane, helicopter, snowshoes, skis, snowmobiles, motorboat, rowboat—any available means of transportation. They have found people living in packing crates, old boxcars, barn lofts, and mine tunnels. Sometimes their dogged pursuit of census returns has led to very strange experiences.

One census taker helped to deliver a baby at an isolated farmhouse when she arrived just as the infant was about to be born. Another got locked in with a chain gang of prison convicts for three hours after a new guard came on duty and refused to believe the census taker was not a prisoner. Yet another census taker once interviewed a farmer who refused to stop plowing long enough to be questioned. She stood in the field and asked him one question each time he passed. It took her two hours to get through the questionnaire.

Today, most Americans never even see an enumerator because their census questionnaire arrives in the mail near

F U N   F A C T S

WHAT WAS THE MOST FAMOUS USE OF CENSUS DATA BY A HISTORIAN?

In 1890, the census found that there was no territory left in the United States with a population density of less than 2 persons per square mile (0.8 square kilometer). The finding was viewed as proof that the frontier was dead. Historian Frederick Jackson Turner used the census data in a famous essay called "The Significance of the Frontier in American History." Turner's essay discussed how America's plentiful unsettled land had given the nation the opportunity to keep expanding westward, a major influence on the national character.

the end of March, and they return it by mail by April 1, Census Day. But in rural areas where the addresses are not precise enough for mailing purposes, a Census Bureau enumerator may be dispatched to visit the people who live there.

By the way, there's a reason that the census is taken in April. At that time of year, schools are in session, fewer people are on vacation, and the severe weather of winter is over. These facts make it easier for enumerators to make their rounds and more likely that Americans will be at home.

FIRST, FIND SOME ADDRESSES . . .

It takes a decade or more to prepare for a decennial census. Numerous planning sessions map out questionnaires. Test runs evaluate methods and procedures. And the Bureau must hire an army of temporary employees to do fieldwork and office work.

One of the most labor-intensive tasks is assembling address lists that are as complete and accurate as possible. The Census Bureau buys residential addresses from direct mail businesses that sell mailing lists. Census and Postal Service workers check and update the address list before mailing labels are produced for the questionnaire envelopes.

Americans live in diverse places. But no matter where their regular place of residence is, that's where they are to be counted for the Decennial Census—in homes or apartments, college dormitories, military barracks, nursing homes, and prisons. To find those who have no roof over their head, the 1990 census sent fieldworkers out at night to count people in shelters and cheap hotels as well as streets, parks, and other public areas. It was the first time the census had gone to such trouble to count the homeless, whose growing numbers had become the focus of public concern and debate.

THE QUESTIONS

The questions have changed from census to census. In the past, census questionnaires have asked American households about very sensitive topics, including insanity, criminal records, the amount of debt they owed, and whether their heads were larger or smaller than average. Since 1940, however, the Decennial Census has been limited to gathering information only on population and housing.

The Decennial Census, or Census of Population and Housing, is actually two censuses in one. The census of population counts how many inhabitants there are and asks about their personal, social, and economic characteristics. The census of housing counts the nation's residential dwellings and takes note of their physical and financial characteristics.

How many questions are asked depends on whether the householder has received the short form or the long form. While the short form asks for basic information—such as each individual's age, sex, race, and marital status—the long form seeks more detail, such as whether a householder has a Ph.D. or how he or she gets to work. Housing questions in the short form might ask how many rooms a house or apartment has, while the long form might ask when the building was erected and whether solar energy is used.

The content of the questionnaire undergoes scrutiny by officials in the legislative and executive branches of the federal government. Congress must be advised of the proposed question topics no later than three years before Census Day. Two years before the census, Congress is required to be given the wording of the questions. Questions in the 1990 census were written by the staff of the Bureau of the Census and then reviewed by the Office of Management of the Budget before they were sent to Congress.

TABULATING THE FINDINGS

In the days following April 1 of a census year, millions of completed questionnaires pour into the bureau's 450-plus temporary district offices or to one of seven processing centers across the country. Processing begins as soon as the questionnaires come in. The questionnaires are checked against address lists to track which areas

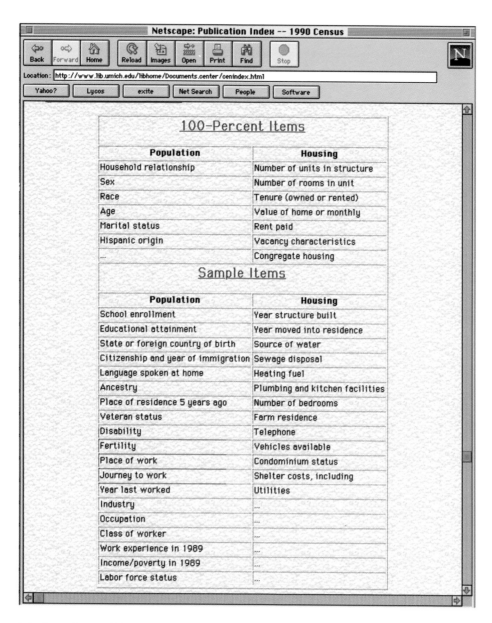

Location: http://www.lib.umich.edu/libhome/Documents.center/cenindex.html

Yahoo?   Lycos   exite   Net Search   People   Software

100-Percent Items

Population	Housing
Household relationship	Number of units in structure
Sex	Number of rooms in unit
Race	Tenure (owned or rented)
Age	Value of home or monthly
Marital status	Rent paid
Hispanic origin	Vacancy characteristics
...	Congregate housing

Sample Items

Population	Housing
School enrollment	Year structure built
Educational attainment	Year moved into residence
State or foreign country of birth	Source of water
Citizenship and year of immigration	Sewage disposal
Language spoken at home	Heating fuel
Ancestry	Plumbing and kitchen facilities
Place of residence 5 years ago	Number of bedrooms
Veteran status	Farm residence
Disability	Telephone
Fertility	Vehicles available
Place of work	Condominium status
Journey to work	Shelter costs, including
Year last worked	Utilities
Industry	...
Occupation	...
Class of worker	...
Work experience in 1989	...
Income/poverty in 1989	...
Labor force status	...

The long form of the census asks a greater number and variety of questions than the short form does.

CD-ROMs and Internet Web sites classify and interpret census results, and make them available to the public.

did not respond and will require an enumerator visit. Questionnaires are also examined for completeness, and follow-up phone calls are made where necessary. Questionnaires that are looked over at the district offices are then packed into trucks, sealed for security, and sent to one of the processing centers.

At the processing centers, the questionnaires are sorted and microfilmed by a high-speed camera, and the film is put through FOSDIC (Film Optical Sensing Device for Input to Computers), a system that transfers the responses to each item on the questionnaire onto computer tape.

Computers transmit the data electronically to Census Bureau headquarters, where tabulating will begin. The only identification in the computer is a geographic code that links the data from each questionnaire with its correct census block.

When the data have been completely tabulated, the paper questionnaires are destroyed. The microfilm is stored under guard at the Personal Census Service Branch in Pittsburg, Kansas. Only the respondent or his or her legal representative can obtain access to the information. A copy is also given to the National Archives, which grants access to researchers after 72 years.

By law, the Department of Commerce must report the total population count by state to the president and the states by December 31 of the decennial year. Detailed population counts by state must be reported to the president and the states by the following April 1.

The Bureau publishes data in several forms. In addition to printed reports on a wide variety of topics, extensive census data is now available via electronic media, including magnetic tapes, CD-ROMs, and online data. In the 1990 census, the Bureau also began offering electronic mapping. There is now an electronic map of the entire United States down to the block level. In other words, you can look at a computer-generated map of the very block that you live on. The system is called TIGER, for Topographically Integrated Geographical Encoding and Referencing.

FUN FACTS

¿HABLA ESPANOL?

In 1990, 31.8 million U.S. residents, or 14 percent of the population five years old and over, reported they spoke a language other than English at home. That's up from 23.1 million persons, or 11 percent, in 1980.

6

STATISTICS, DEMOGRAPHY, AND GEOGRAPHY

How many new mothers are in the workforce compared to mothers of grown children? What part of the country is growing the fastest? Are minorities becoming the nation's new majority?

Painting a statistical portrait of the United States requires much more than an ability to count really big numbers. In every activity it undertakes, the Census Bureau uses the established principles and methods of statistics. Statistics is the science of collecting, classifying, analyzing, and interpreting numerical facts or data. It's a way of making sure that numbers represent useful and meaningful information.

The science of statistics is a relatively new field, dating from about the 17th century. Statisticians did not begin to develop rules for collecting data until the late 19th or early 20th century. By the end of the 19th century, census data was attracting growing interest from business associations, social reformers, and academic researchers. As the census's value became apparent, statisticians began to have a say in determining which questions should be asked and how to ask them.

Demographics is a social science that uses statistics for the scientific study of the size, distribution, and makeup of populations and the changes that occur in populations over time. The social scientists who study demographics are called demographers. They measure population change by examining births, deaths, and movement. Birth and death rates are expressed as the number of births or deaths per 1,000 population in a given year. Movement is internal migration and international migration. Internal migration is the movement of people within a country, such as across a county line; international migration refers to the relocating of people from one nation to another. Both have played an important role in the history of our country, and they continue to define our national character.

STATISTICAL METHODOLOGIES

Professional data processors and statisticians have developed some standard techniques for analyzing data. Sometimes, for example, data may be expressed as a "mean," as in "mean" family income. The "mean" is a mathematical term for what most people call an average. When the total of all income reported by all families is divided by the number of families, the result is the mean family income. But statisticians also calculate another kind of value called a "median," which can be more useful than a mean in understanding population patterns. The median income for families would be the middle figure in a sequence of income numbers, with an equal number of numbers above and below it. In a group of people aged 1, 5, 6, 20, 38, 43, and 49, the median age would be 20.

Precise terminology is very important to statisticians and to those who want to use statistical data. Even terms that seem obvious must be precisely defined.

FUN FACTS

WHO'S DROPPING OUT?

According to the 1990 census, about 11 percent of 16–19-year-olds have dropped out of school. Nevada had the highest dropout rate, at 15 percent. The lowest was North Dakota, at 4.6 percent.

For example, it might seem that a household and a family would mean the same thing. In fact, to the Census Bureau those are very different things. A family refers to all persons who occupy a single housing unit and who are related to the person who owns or rents the home. A household is a group of people who live in a housing unit, whether they are related or not. The Census Bureau then classifies households as either family or nonfamily households.

When questionnaires are used to gather demographic data, it's critical to follow standard statistical procedures. Statisticians have developed methodologies for crafting interview questions so that they are worded clearly and carefully. The Census Bureau also takes pains to assure that its questions are phrased in a manner that won't offend any respondent. How the questionnaire is administered is equally important. The Census Bureau follows established procedures for determining the size and the composition of the group of people to be questioned.

SAMPLING

To understand the census, you must understand the difference between censuses and surveys. While a census is a complete count of every member of a group or population, a survey, or sample, examines a smaller segment of the whole group. When it would take too long or cost too much to count every member of a population, sampling is a convenient way to gather information. As census people are fond of explaining, "The doctor doesn't have to drain all of the blood from your body to find out your blood type."

Done properly, a survey can produce accurate estimates about the larger population. The size of the sample is important, as is the method of selection. Often surveys select people randomly, such as by picking every sixth name on an address list. Of course, the information collected through a sample of a population is subject to a certain amount of uncertainty or error. Statisticians use the term *sampling error* to discuss the uncertainty element. The larger the sample, the smaller the amount of error.

The Census Bureau's Decennial Census uses both census and survey methodologies. The short form of the questionnaire is a census because it is received by everyone; the long form questionnaire, which was sent to one in six households in

1990, is a survey. Our government uses the census for the actual population count, and the sampling method to find out about specific characteristics of the population.

THE IMPORTANCE OF GEOGRAPHY

There's a "where" in every statistic. In other words, whenever someone uses census data to investigate a problem or question, geography matters.

Suppose you own a chain of toy stores. You might like to know how many babies were born last year. But you'd also like to know *where* most of those babies were born, so you can decide where you should build new stores.

UNITED STATES REGIONS, DIVISONS AND STATES

The Census Bureau divides the United States into a number of districts and regions.

Most people think of the country's geographic units as the ones defined by law—the states, counties, cities, townships, and American Indian reservations. The census provides data for those areas, but it also uses statistics to define other geographic units. They range from large areas, such as regions and divisions, down to small areas, such as census tracts and blocks. The entire nation is divided into four regions, each containing two or three divisions. The divisions are made up of states.

Statisticians often talk about "metropolitan areas" instead of cities. Generally, a metropolitan area includes a sizable city with its suburbs, and has a total population of at least 100,000. But a metropolitan area can also consist of an entire county, particularly in parts of the country outside New England, where cities and towns are the population centers. A Standard Metropolitan Statistical Area (SMSA) usually consists of a central city with a population of more than 50,000, the county or counties in which it is located, and the other counties that border it and are socially and economically connected to the central city.

More than half of the U.S. population lives in metropolitan areas of over one million, according to the 1990 census. In 1990, there were 40 metropolitan areas with at least one million residents. The largest area, with 18 million people, is the NY-NJ-CT-PA CMSA, or Consolidated Metropolitan Statistical Area.

As far the cities themselves, here are the nation's top five cities and their 1990 populations:

- New York, NY—7,323,000
- Los Angeles, CA—3,486,000
- Chicago, IL—2,784,000
- Houston, TX— 1,631,000
- Philadelphia, PA—1,586,000

More than 16 million people live in the five largest cities of the United States.

7

PUTTING
THE NUMBERS
TO WORK

 A journalist pores over a census report on an interesting new population trend: Black people in northern cities are rediscovering their roots and moving back to the South in growing numbers.

 Government health and housing agencies concerned about lead poisoning analyze census data to pinpoint housing units built before 1960 when lead paint was widely used. They also use census data to determine how many children live in those areas.

 A historian studying military pensions threads a microfilm reel through a machine at the National Archives to view the 1890 Special Census of Union Veterans and Widows.

 A company that specializes in data analysis buys census information and analyzes the numbers for a customer considering whether to build a factory in a particular place.

Census reports provide data on families, creating fascinating glimpses into changes in American life.

Those are just a few of the multitude of uses for Census Bureau data by government, private businesses, journalists, social scientists, and nonprofit organizations. Because the Bureau collects data throughout the country from year to year and from generation to generation, its statistics are often used for comparative studies.

The Census Bureau delivers data in a variety of ways. It publishes numerous printed reports and maps, and in recent years it has been producing electronic products through CD-ROM technology and online services. Perhaps the single most useful collection of data is the Bureau's Statistical Abstract. Published every year since 1878, the Statistical Abstract includes data on over 30 topics covering the nation's demographic, social, economic, and political makeup.

F U N   F A C T S

WHERE IS THE CENTER OF POPULATION?

The "center of population" is the point at which the United States would balance perfectly if it were a flat surface and everyone weighed an equal amount. The center has shifted westward, and recently, southward, as shown by the map below

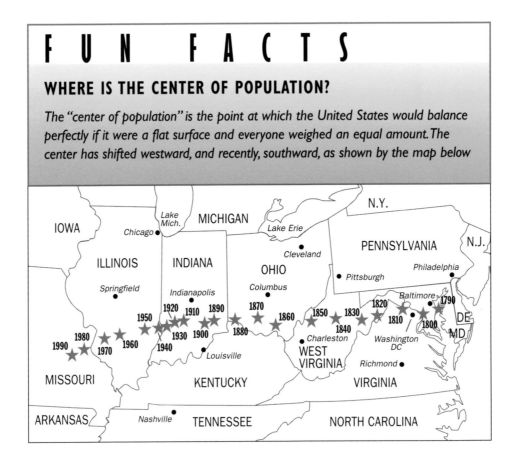

Most of the data collected and tabulated by the Census Bureau is available for free. The Bureau also sells data to businesses or other organizations that need special tabulations or more detailed presentations. The bureau's printed census and survey reports are available for free through the Federal Depository Library System, a network of more than 1,400 libraries nationwide. Other sources include 1,600 State Data Centers throughout the country. Public libraries and academic libraries may have the reports in their collections or have access to them. Increasingly, the reports are also available on microfiche or computer tape.

The Internet is the wave of the future for delivering Census Bureau data and statistics. On its World Wide Web site (http://www.census.gov), the Census Bureau offers a treasure trove of information for Internet users. Computer users can view maps, ask the experts questions, or browse through statistical summaries on a variety of topics. There's even an up-to-the-minute estimate of the nation's population. Ultimately, the Census Bureau hopes to deliver most of its data and statistics through the Internet and electronic systems. The benefits are many. For users, the Internet puts vast amounts of data within the reach of a few computer keyboard strokes. For the Bureau, reporting census and survey data is much faster and cheaper on the Internet than in printed materials.

APPORTIONMENT

The primary purpose of the census remains Congressional apportionment, which was the original purpose for conducting a nationwide census. On or before December 31 of the census year, the Census Bureau sends its official census counts and apportion calculations for each state to the president. The president then provides those figures to the Congress. If the House decides to make any changes, it must pass legislation. The Senate must agree, and the president must then sign or veto it. The clerk of the House informs each state governor of the number of representatives to which the state is entitled.

The number of representatives per state is based on three factors:

✍ The population, as determined by the Decennial Census. For the 1990 census, the state population totals included the resident population of each state, plus people in the military and federal government who lived overseas.

✍ The number of members in the House of Representatives, as determined by Congress. That number has been 435 since 1911, except for a temporary increase to 437 in 1959 when Alaska and Hawaii became states.

✍ A method of calculation set by Congress. It would seem that the easiest approach would be to figure out what each state's percentage of the total population is. However, that could result in fractions of a representative, and a state cannot send a fraction of an elected official to Washington. Also, the Constitution says that every state is entitled to at least one representative regardless of its population. That means that 50 of the 435 seats are already allocated, and the census count is actually determining how to divide the remaining 385 seats among the 50 states.

The method for calculating the apportionment has changed five times since 1790. Since 1941, apportionment has been calculated with a complex mathematical formula called the Method of Equal Proportions. This method assigns seats in the House of Representatives according to a priority value. To get the priority value, the population of a state is multiplied by a special number called a multiplier.

Following the 1990 Census, 21 states lost or gained representatives in the House of Representatives. Eight states—Arizona, California, Florida, Georgia, North Carolina, Texas, Virginia, and Washington—gained because their population rose.

Thirteen states lost seats. These states were Illinois, Iowa, Kansas, Kentucky, Louisiana, Massachusetts, Michigan, Montana, New Jersey, New York, Ohio, Pennsylvania, and West Virginia.

After it is determined how many seats each state has, the state legislatures must draw new congressional district boundaries. That process is known as redistricting. Current law requires that the population of those districts

F U N   F A C T S

HOW IS THE MINORITY POPULATION EXPECTED TO GROW?

The African American share of the total U.S. population is expected to increase from 12.6 percent in 1995 to 12.9 percent in 2000, 14.2 percent in 2025, and 15.4 percent in 2050.

should be made as equal as possible, and plans should not be drawn so as to discriminate against a specific segment of the population. Detailed census results are used for redistricting.

THE PRIVACY ISSUE

By law, the information collected by the Census Bureau is used only for statistical purposes. No information that could identify a person or business can be released.

Census Bureau employees must swear under oath that they will not disclose any information about individuals or businesses gathered by the agency. Violations are punishable by up to five years in jail and a fine of up to $5,000.

In addition, the names and addresses of people interviewed for censuses or surveys are kept separate from the computer tapes containing their answers. If a geographic area is so small that statistics could be used to identify someone, the Bureau withholds those numbers.

But the privacy of respondents hasn't always been protected. In the first census of 1790, the census-takers posted their results in public places for all to see. The purpose was so that omissions and inaccuracies could be corrected.

The Census Act for 1880 was the first legislation prohibiting census workers from disclosing information. The counters were required to take an oath not to disclose any information they collected except to their supervisors.

Here are some of the controversial ways in which census data were used—some might say abused—over the years:

✍ As debates over slavery raged in the mid-19th century, a prominent American statesman named Henry Clay suggested that the government should send all blacks to Liberia, the new African republic established by some freed U.S. slaves. Clay used the census count to determine how many ships would be needed.

✍ During the Civil War, Union General William T. Sherman led his troops through Georgia's plantation country, living off the land by seizing food

Members of the House of Representatives listen to the President's State of the Union address. The number of representatives each state sends to the House is determined by census results.

from the farms they passed. He used 1860 census data on crops and livestock to map troop routes.

✎ In World War I, the Justice Department prosecuted men who did not register for military service. Census records were used to prove the men's ages.

✎ In World War II, the War Department wanted to send people of Japanese origin to internment camps. The Census Bureau refused a request for 1940 census records showing the names and addresses of Japanese living in western states. But it did turn over stacks of punch cards (which had no names or addresses) identifying those persons by census tract or other small area, since this information was already available to the public in published reports.

GENEALOGICAL RESEARCH

Many people who want to research their ancestry turn to old census records in order to map their family tree.

Schedules become available for public view after 72 years. At this writing, census schedules from 1790 to 1920 are available for public view at the National Archives in Washington, D.C., or at its 11 regional archives. The schedules available for researchers are copies of the actual forms filled out for every family or household. Many libraries, state archives, historical societies, and genealogical libraries operated by the Church of Jesus Christ of Latter Day Saints also maintain collections of census microfilms.

The 1790–1840 schedules give the names of the head of household only. Beginning in 1850, names of all household members were listed. Records from two censuses have been destroyed by fire. During the War of 1812, the British burned up 1790 schedules

FUN FACTS

WHO'S GOING FOR BROKE?

Some 973,000 Americans declared bankruptcy in 1992, up from 360,000 in 1981. California led with over 152,000 bankruptcies, followed by Florida with 52,000.

A librarian shows a woman how to look up census records on a microfilm machine.

from six states or territories. Practically all of the 1890 census schedules were destroyed by a fire in 1921.

Searching microfilm reels for information on a particular family can be very time consuming. The reels are arranged by decade, then by state and county, which means a researcher must know where the person in question lived at the time of the census. Many records are not indexed, and it can be difficult to decipher microfilmed versions of the old handwritten ledgers whose ink has grown faint.

Still, locating an ancestor in official census records from long ago is a thrill that keeps many genealogists doggedly pursuing their quarry of data.

8

CENSUS
2000

When the United States looks in the mirror at the dawn of the new century, what will it see? There's no question that the 2000 Decennial will be bigger than ever. But many people are demanding that it also be better than ever.

It takes years to plan the nationwide Decennial. Bureau officials began planning for 2000 even before the 1990 Decennial questionnaires went out. They had three goals: faster, less costly, and more accurate.

The stakes are high. As always, billions of dollars of federal money will be divided based on the data that's collected from America's 119 million households. The census results will also influence who gets elected to the House of Representatives in the 2000 election—and, possibly, which party controls the House. But the Bureau's plans for 2000 have received added scrutiny because of controversy that arose over the 1990 census.

There was widespread dissatisfaction with the 1990 census. Critics said it cost too much and accomplished too little. The 1990 census cost $2.6 billion. Some 500,000 census-takers had to hit the streets to look for people when the mail-in responses dropped to 65 percent, down from 75 percent in 1980. Sometimes enumerators had to go back to neighborhoods two or three times. Even so, the final count didn't satisfy everyone. The Census Bureau was criticized for missing as many as five million people. Twenty-one lawsuits were filed over the 1990 census by various states and cities challenging the results.

With so much controversy, it was no surprise that Census 2000 began attracting attention even before the ink was dry on the 1990 census reports.

THE UNDERCOUNT

Of the millions of Americans who were overlooked in the 1990 census, most were poor, black, or Hispanic. Some of those who were missed didn't want to be counted. Perhaps they distrusted government or had something to hide. Others simply weren't found by the Bureau's enumerators. It has been reported that the census overlooked 1.8 percent of the U.S. population, including 4.4 percent of the black population and 5 percent of Hispanics.

To improve the accuracy of the count, the Census Bureau has proposed a new plan in 2000: "nonresponse sampling." In the past, the Bureau attempted to complete a questionnaire for every household. For those who didn't mail in a questionnaire, the enumerators attempted to find them and fill one out, or fill one out on their behalf by interviewing neighbors. Under the new plan, the Bureau would aim to reach 90 percent of the population using the traditional census-taking methods. For the remaining households, the Bureau would use sampling—collecting responses from a proportion of the entire group of nonrespondents—and use the resulting estimates to round out the count to 100 percent.

The new approach is controversial. Critics say it is unconstitutional because it is not the "actual enumeration" that the Constitution requires. They also charge that it could make political manipulation of the numbers easier.

The Bureau maintains that accuracy, not the method used, fulfills the Bureau's Constitutional obligations. Ultimately, the matter could be decided by the courts.

YOUR GENERATION

Some of the most interesting data to come out of Census 2000 is likely to look at the trends that affect you, your friends, and the rest of your generation.

Some 63 million Americans were 18 and younger in 1990. That could grow to rival the 76 million Americans in the baby boom, the generation born in the years after World War II. The baby boom left its imprint on our society in the second half of the 20th century. Your generation will wield similar influence in the next century.

Here are some of the demographic characteristics that set your generation apart from the baby boomers:

✍ More multiracial. In 1990, there were nearly two million children under 18 who were "of a different race than one or both of their parents." The numbers translate into about one mixed-race child for every 35 Americans under 18—slightly more than one to every school classroom.

✍ More divorces. Today's young people are less likely to live with two parents than their baby-boom predecessors were. In 1970, 85 percent of children under age 18 lived with two parents and 12 percent lived with one parent. By 1995, only 69 percent of children lived with two parents, and 27 percent lived with a single parent.

✍ Sex roles. Shifts in the roles of men and women have brought about major changes in our society in recent decades. For example, many more of today's children have mothers who work. In 1990, 72 percent of the children who lived with their mothers had mothers who worked for pay.

GETTING THE PUBLIC'S ATTENTION

How do you get people to respond? For Census 2000, the Bureau plans an all-out assault to make the public aware of how important participation in the census is. Households who need to be reminded to mail in their forms cost six times as much as those who do not. It costs up to 18 times as much to use field staff to track down the missing respondents.

For 2000, the Bureau is designing user-friendly forms that are easier to read and fill out. With junk mail so common, mailings must be eye-catching to grab the attention of busy Americans. Before the actual forms go out, the Bureau may also mail out letters notifying Americans that a questionnaire is coming soon. There may also be a major advertising campaign aimed at convincing Americans that filling out a census questionnaire is the patriotic thing to do.

Mail-out/mail-back technique will still be important in 2000, but it may not be the only way the Bureau reaches people. Americans might pick up a census form at the mall, at school, or in other spots around their communities. They might also be able to respond via a toll-free telephone call or on the Internet.

TECHNOLOGY

Technology will play the biggest role yet in Census 2000. In 1990, the census was microfilmed and keypunched. In 2000, the Bureau will use computers that can read handwriting to convert completed forms directly to computer files ready for tabulation. Sophisticated software will allow the Bureau to spot duplications in case a household mistakenly files multiple responses.

Data users will also benefit from better technology. In the past, a user may have had to thumb through thick books of statistical tables to get what he or she needed. In 2000, the data will be available on the Internet in a fashion that will allow people to point and click their computer mouse to access the information they want.

Some of the most interesting data to come out of Census 2000 is likely to paint a portrait of your generation.

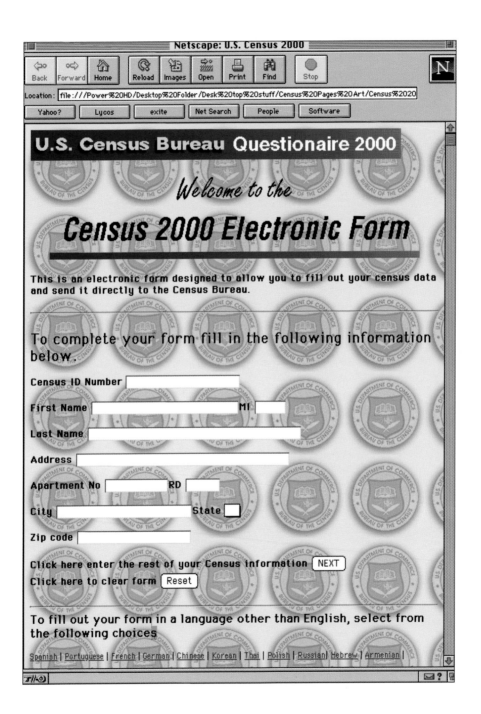

Netscape: U.S. Census 2000

Back | Forward | Home | Reload | Images | Open | Print | Find | Stop

N

Location: file:///Power%20HD/Desktop%20Folder/Desk%20top%20stuff/Census%20Pages%20Art/Census%2020

Yahoo? | Lycos | exite | Net Search | People | Software

U.S. Census Bureau Questionaire 2000

Welcome to the

Census 2000 Electronic Form

This is an electronic form designed to allow you to fill out your census data and send it directly to the Census Bureau.

To complete your form fill in the following information below.

Census ID Number

First Name   MI

Last Name

Address

Apartment No   RD

City   State

Zip code

Click here enter the rest of your Census information NEXT
Click here to clear form Reset

To fill out your form in a language other than English, select from the following choices

Spanish | Portuguese | French | German | Chinese | Korean | Thai | Polish | Russian | Hebrew | Armenian |

In keeping with its traditional long-range focus, the Census Bureau is already looking ahead to the next century's head counts. In 2010, the Bureau would like to phase out its often criticized long-form questionnaire and replace it with a new American Community Survey.

The long form has grown in recent decades as Congress has ordered new questions to gather data for various federal programs. In 1990, the long form had 20 pages and up to 60 questions. Americans were asked such things as whether their homes had toilets that flush, how much their mortgage payments were, and what time they left the house for work.

The American Community Survey would be a large monthly household survey conducted using mailed questionnaires, telephone interviews, and visits from Bureau field representatives. Because the new information would become available every year, it would be more accurate and more timely than decennial survey data. The Census Bureau is already putting the concept to the test.

One thing won't change. Enumerators will still be a vital part of the Census Bureau's fact-finding. Those foot soldiers will still be dispatched to every corner of the nation to see that everyone is counted.

In the future, Americans might be able to
fill out census questionnaires on the Internet.

GLOSSARY

Census—A count, or enumeration, of every member of a group of people or things in a given area.

Data—Statistics, pieces of information, a group or body of facts.

Decennial—Done every ten years. Often used to refer to the Census Bureau's Decennial Census of Population and Housing.

Demographics—A social science that studies the characteristics of a population and how they change over time.

Enumerator—A person who counts the population for a census.

Mean—An average number.

Median—The middle figure in a sequence of numbers, with an equal number of numbers above and below it.

Statistics—The science of collecting, classifying, analyzing, and interpreting numerical facts.

Survey—A count of a portion, or sample, of a population. When done accurately, a survey provides important generalizations about a larger population.

INDEX